INTRODUCTION: VISION OF THE FUTURE

Generative Artificial Intelligence (AI) is emerging as a transformative force in the corporate landscape, promising to redefine not only how we work, but also how we think about the future of business. This technology, which enables machines to create new and meaningful content, is rapidly spreading across all sectors, from finance to manufacturing, from marketing to customer service.

The Transformative Potential of Generative AI

According to recent studies by Harvard Business Review, generative AI is set to transform more than 40 per cent of all jobs, with the greatest impact in the legal, banking, insurance and capital markets sectors. This revolution is driven by deep learning models that can process huge amounts of unstructured data, opening up new possibilities for automation and innovation. Generative AI is radically transforming all kinds of jobs, making AI accessible to almost anyone, using everyday language commands instead of code. The skills needed to excel in this new era of collaboration between humans and AI include intelligent questioning, integration of judgement and mutual apprenticeship.

Innovative Strategies for Business, Overview

The strategies for integrating Generative AI into business are manifold and require a holistic approach. McKinsey & Company points out that Generative AI could add between $2.6 and $4.4 trillion in annual value, redefining the way people work and live. Leading companies are already leveraging this technology to gain a competitive advantage, implementing AI solutions ranging from personalising the customer experience to optimising production processes. The adoption of Generative AI has seen a significant spike and is beginning to generate tangible value for organisations.

CHAPTER 1: THE STRATEGIC REVOLUTION OF GENERATIVE AI

The adoption of Generative AI in companies is driven by a series of strategies aimed at harnessing its potential to transform work activities and business models. According to the Harvard Business Review, Generative AI is set to transform over 40 per cent of all work activities, with a particularly significant impact in the legal, banking, insurance and capital markets sectors. This prediction is based on the ability of Generative AI to process commands in everyday language rather than code, making it accessible to a wider audience.

Training and Skills Development: The adoption of generative AI is transforming the work landscape, requiring a new set of skills, known as 'fusion skills'. These skills are essential to interact effectively with large language models (LLMs) such as ChatGPT.

Intelligent Interrogation: This competence involves the ability to formulate questions to AI so that it produces better reasoning and results. For example, a customer service representative might use it to find the answer to a complex customer query.

Judgment Integration: This is about integrating human discernment when a Generative AI model is uncertain about what to do or lacks the necessary business or ethical context in its reasoning.

Reciprocal Apprenticing: This skill helps AI to learn specific business tasks and needs by incorporating rich data and organisational knowledge into its instructions, training it to become a cocreator.

Companies are responding to these needs through

targeted training programmes and investments in technology infrastructure. A global survey by McKinsey revealed that 65 per cent of respondents reported that their organisations are using Generative AI on a regular basis, almost double the percentage from just ten months earlier. This demonstrates a rapid increase in the adoption of Generative AI and underscores the importance of developing the skills needed to harness this technology.

Companies also face significant challenges, such as a lack of expertise and concerns about privacy and security. To overcome these barriers, it is crucial that training programmes convey not only technical knowledge, but also raise awareness of ethical and legal issues related to the use of AI.

In conclusion, training and skills development in the area of Generative AI are crucial for companies that want to stay ahead of the curve and take advantage of the opportunities offered by this emerging technology. Through targeted investments and innovative training programmes, companies can turn challenges into opportunities, harnessing Generative AI to improve productivity and stimulate creativity. Technology Integration: To implement Generative AI, companies are building robust and flexible technology infrastructures. This often requires strategic partnerships and significant investments in hardware and software.

Culture of Innovation: Generative AI adoption requires a corporate culture that embraces change and innovation. Successful companies are creating environments where exploration and adoption of new technologies are encouraged.

These strategies are critical for companies wishing to remain competitive and take advantage of the opportunities offered by Generative AI. Through training, infrastructure and culture, companies can transform their operations and business models, leveraging Generative AI to personalise the customer experience, optimise processes and accelerate innovation.

Infrastructure and Platforms

The technology infrastructure for the integration of Generative AI is a crucial aspect that companies must carefully consider. A robust and scalable platform is crucial to support the implementation and operation of Generative AI models. Companies must evaluate the available options, taking into account factors such as compatibility with existing systems, ease of use, long-term support and security.

The selection of the right platform is guided by a thorough evaluation of the company's specific needs. This process includes analysing the required technical capabilities, such as handling large volumes of data and the ability to process complex requests in real time. In addition, platforms must be able to support the continuous evolution of generative AI models and adapt to new challenges emerging in the technological landscape.

A key element for technology integration is the creation of a model hub, which contains trained and approved models ready to be implemented on demand. This hub should include standard APIs that act as bridges to connect Generative AI models to applications or business data. Context management and caching are equally important, as they accelerate processing by providing models with relevant information from enterprise data sources.

Companies must also consider the importance of effective IT governance to ensure that the integration of Generative AI is aligned with corporate policies and industry regulations. This includes setting standards for data quality, security and privacy, as well as creating a governance framework that oversees the ethical and responsible use of Generative AI.

In conclusion, the infrastructure and platforms for integrating

Generative AI represent a strategic investment for companies. Through careful planning and the selection of appropriate technologies, companies can make the most of the opportunities offered by this emerging technology to transform their business processes and gain a significant competitive advantage.

AI Readiness Assessment

The AI readiness assessment is a critical step for companies wishing to integrate Generative AI into their processes. This assessment helps determine whether the organisation has the capabilities, resources and infrastructure to effectively exploit Generative AI.

Business Process Analysis

Companies must start with a thorough analysis of their current business processes. This includes identifying areas where Generative AI can bring the most value and identifying any infrastructure or skills gaps that could hinder integration. The analysis should also consider how Generative AI might affect existing workflows and what changes might be needed to facilitate a smooth transition.

Evaluation of Staff Competences

Another key aspect is the assessment of staff competencies. Companies need to ensure that their employees have the necessary skills to work with generative AI or that there is a plan in place to develop these skills through training. This includes understanding AI models, the ability to formulate effective requests, and knowledge of the ethical and legal implications of using AI.

Implications of IA on Existing Operations

Companies must also consider the implications of AI on existing operations. This includes analysing the impact that generative AI could have on productivity, service quality and customer satisfaction. In addition, it is important to assess potential risks, such as data security and privacy, and develop plans to mitigate them.

Conclusion

Assessing AI readiness is a complex process that requires detailed analysis and a holistic approach. Through this assessment, companies can identify the key areas they need to focus on to ensure a successful integration of generative AI and make the most of its potential.

Development of an Advanced AI Roadmap

The development of an advanced AI roadmap is essential for companies wishing to successfully integrate Generative AI. A well-defined roadmap guides the organisation through the integration process, ensuring that each step is aligned with the business objectives and capabilities of Generative AI.

Definition of Strategic Objectives

The roadmap must begin with the definition of the company's strategic objectives. These goals may include increasing operational efficiency, improving the customer experience or accelerating innovation. The goals must be specific, measurable, achievable, relevant and time-bound (SMART) to ensure that the roadmap is practical and achievable.

Capacity and Resource Analysis

A thorough analysis of the company's current capabilities and resources is crucial to determine the focus areas of the roadmap. This includes an analysis of personnel skills, existing technological infrastructure and available financial resources for the integration of Generative AI.

Planning Integration Phases

The roadmap must outline the stages of integration of generative AI, from initial prototyping and testing to full-scale implementation. Each phase must include clear milestones, assigned responsibilities and success metrics to monitor progress.

Adaptability and Scalability

The roadmap must be adaptable and scalable to respond to future developments in the AI landscape. Companies must be ready to modify their strategy according to new developments in the field of generative AI and changing market needs.

Conclusion

An advanced AI roadmap is a vital element in the integration of generative AI in companies. It provides a framework for navigating the integration process, ensuring that the organisation is ready to exploit the opportunities offered by this emerging technology.

Redefining Business Models with Generative AI

The redefinition of business models through Generative AI is a process that is transforming the way companies create value and interact with customers and markets. This section explores how Generative AI is affecting three key areas: mass customisation, process optimisation and product innovation.

Mass Customisation with Generative AI

Mass customisation is one of the most significant transformations that generative AI is bringing to the business world. Companies are using AI to deliver highly personalised experiences to a vast number of customers, a task that would have been impossible or extremely expensive with traditional methods.

Innovative Approach to Customisation

Generative AI makes it possible to analyse customer data in real time and generate personalised content that responds to their preferences and behaviours. This level of personalisation can significantly increase customer engagement and brand loyalty[5].

Successful Examples

An example of success in this area is ecommerce companies using generative AI to create customised product descriptions or to recommend products based on users' browsing behaviour. This not only improves the shopping experience, but can also lead to an increase in conversions and average order value.

Challenges and Considerations

Despite the benefits, mass customisation with generative AI also presents challenges. Companies must ensure that they manage customer data responsibly and maintain transparency on how it is used. In addition, they must be able to integrate Generative AI into their existing systems without disrupting current operations.

In conclusion, mass customisation with generative AI is redefining the way companies interact with customers, offering unprecedented opportunities to create unique and engaging experiences. Companies that manage to harness this technology ethically and strategically can expect to gain a significant competitive advantage in their industry.

In conclusion, mass customisation with generative AI is redefining the way companies interact with customers, offering unprecedented opportunities to create unique and engaging experiences. Companies that manage to harness this technology ethically and strategically can expect to gain a significant competitive advantage in their industry.

Application of Generative AI in Financial Services

The integration of generative AI in the financial services sector is having a significant impact, offering new opportunities for innovation and personalisation of services. We look in detail at some of the most relevant applications and case studies that demonstrate the transformative potential of this technology.

Risk Management and Credit Assessment

Generative AI is revolutionising risk management and credit assessment in financial institutions. Using advanced predictive models, banks can analyse transaction patterns in real time to identify suspicious behaviour and prevent fraudulent activities[13]. In addition, generative AI is being used to develop more sophisticated credit scoring systems that take into account a wider range of variables and historical data to provide more accurate assessments[17].

Optimising Banking Services

Banks are using Generative AI to optimise banking services, improving operational efficiency and reducing costs. For example, Generative AI can be used to automate the document verification process or to provide personalised financial advice through virtual assistants.

Successful Case Studies

AlphaSense Assistant: This generative AI tool provides financial analysis and market insights, helping analysts make informed decisions based on up-to-date data and insights.

TallierLT AI @ Morgan Stanley: A platform that harnesses generative AI to optimise trading strategies by analysing large volumes of market data to identify investment opportunities.

ZAML Platform: This solution uses generative AI to improve credit risk assessment by combining traditional and non-traditional data to provide a more comprehensive risk assessment.

Ethical and Safety Considerations

With the adoption of generative AI, ethical and security issues also arise. Financial institutions need to ensure that AI models are free of bias and that customer data is handled securely and in compliance with privacy regulations.

In conclusion, Generative AI is offering financial institutions powerful tools to improve risk management, personalise services and optimise operations. The highlighted case studies demonstrate how Generative AI can be harnessed to gain competitive advantages and innovate in the financial services industry.

Customisation and Inventory Management

In the retail sector, Generative AI is transforming both the customer experience and the internal management of operations. Here is an in-depth look at how Generative AI is affecting these two crucial aspects of retail.

Customer customisation

Generative AI is enabling retailers to offer an unprecedented level of personalisation. For example, a clothing chain could use AI to analyse customer purchase data and generate personalised style recommendations. This not only improves the customer shopping experience, but also increases the likelihood of repeat purchases. A relevant case study is that of Stitch Fix, a subscription service that uses AI to curate and personalise outfits for its customers based on their feedback and preferences.

Inventory Management

Generative AI is also improving inventory management. For example, a large supermarket chain could employ AI to predict demand for specific products, thereby optimising stock levels and reducing waste. A concrete example is Walmart, which uses AI to manage inventory levels and predict demand more accurately, reducing costs and improving product availability.

Conclusion

These examples demonstrate how Generative AI is giving retailers powerful tools to innovate, improve efficiency and deliver personalised experiences to their customers. Companies adopting Generative AI are discovering new ways to remain competitive and meet evolving consumer expectations.

Advanced Applications of Generative AI in the Telecommunications Sector

In the telecommunications industry, Generative AI is emerging as a revolutionary technology, with applications ranging from network management to customer service personalisation. We examine some of the most advanced applications and case studies that illustrate the impact of Generative AI in this sector.

Optimising Network Operations

Telecommunications companies are using generative AI to monitor and manage network operations more efficiently. For example, AI can analyse network traffic data to identify and prevent potential outages before they occur[1]. In addition, Generative AI is being used for predictive maintenance, enabling companies to predict failures and plan maintenance interventions proactively.

Improved Customer Service

Generative AI is transforming customer service in the telecommunications industry. Advanced chatbots can handle a wide range of customer queries, providing personalised answers and immediate assistance. This not only improves the customer experience, but also reduces the workload on service centres.

Successful Case Studies

Vodafone and Microsoft: Vodafone collaborated with Microsoft to exploit Generative AI through GitHub Copilot to test code writing. During tests with 250 developers, Vodafone experienced a productivity increase of between 30% and 45%.

AT&T: AT&T is using generative AI for network optimisation and troubleshooting, significantly improving the efficiency of network operations.

Conclusion

Generative AI is giving the telecommunications industry powerful tools to optimise network operations, improve customer service and innovate in the services offered. Companies adopting this technology are discovering new ways to remain competitive and meet customer expectations in a rapidly changing market.

CHAPTER 2: VISIONS OF GROWTH WITH GENERATIVE AI

Generative AI is emerging as a catalytic force in the corporate landscape, offering new perspectives for growth and innovation. This technology does not just improve existing processes, but paves the way for new business models, personalised customer experiences and never-before-seen modes of interaction.

Companies adopting Generative AI are finding that they can radically transform their operations, becoming more agile, efficient and future-oriented. This chapter will explore the growth opportunities offered by Generative AI, examining case studies of companies that have successfully implemented these technologies. From innovation strategies driven by corporate culture to the potential economic impact, we will see how Generative AI is shaping the future of business.

With Generative AI, organisations can harness the speed and granularity of technology to identify new growth opportunities, creating a formidable competitive advantage. In this context, innovation becomes a primary driver of growth and resilience, essential to thrive in a rapidly changing world.

In the following pages, we will dive into concrete examples illustrating how Generative AI is transforming sectors such as financial services, healthcare, manufacturing and beyond, highlighting how companies are using this technology to reinvent themselves and grow in previously unimaginable ways.

Prospects for Growth with Generative AI: Innovation and Economic Impact

Generative AI is opening up new frontiers in the business world, promising to be an engine of growth and transformation for companies in various sectors. The growth prospects offered by this technology are vast and can be explored through different application areas.

Innovation in Products and Services

Generative AI enables companies to innovate rapidly in their products and services. For example, in the financial sector, Generative AI is being used to develop new models for forecasting and risk analysis, which can lead to better resource management and more personalised services. This type of innovation not only improves the customer experience, but can also open up new markets and create untapped growth opportunities.

Operational Efficiency and Cost Reduction

Generative AI can increase operational efficiency while reducing costs. For example, automated decision-making and data management can significantly reduce the time and resources required for day-to-day operations, allowing companies to reinvest in other areas of growth.

Successful Case Studies

Morgan Stanley: The financial services firm is testing generative AI to help its financial advisers better harness insights from more than 100,000 research reports.

Government of Iceland: In collaboration with OpenAI, the Icelandic government is using Generative AI to preserve the

Icelandic language, demonstrating how AI can have a cultural as well as an economic impact.

Global Economic Impact

McKinsey research found that the features of generative AI could add up to $4.4 trillion to the global economy annually, underlining its potential as the next productivity front.

Expanding Markets and New Opportunities

Generative AI is enabling companies to explore new markets and identify unexpected growth opportunities. For example, in the insurance industry, Generative AI is being used to analyse emerging risk patterns and develop customised insurance products that address specific customer needs. This proactive approach not only improves customer satisfaction, but also opens up new market segments for insurance companies.

Optimising the Value Chain

Companies are using Generative AI to optimise the entire value chain, from production to distribution. In the manufacturing sector, for example, Generative AI helps predict product demand, optimise inventory levels and improve production planning. This operational efficiency translates into reduced costs and improved customer service.

Successful Case Studies

BMW Group: Using Generative AI, BMW optimised its design processes, significantly reducing the time needed to develop new vehicle models.

Netflix: Generative AI was employed by Netflix to personalise content recommendations for users, improving engagement and increasing subscriber retention.

Sectoral Economic Impact

Generative AI has the potential to significantly influence the economy of entire sectors. According to a study by PwC, AI could contribute up to $15.7 trillion to the global economy by 2030, with Generative AI playing a key role in this increase.

Generative AI is not just a technological innovation; it is a strategic lever that is redefining the concept of growth in the corporate landscape. In the third part of this analysis, we explore how Generative AI is affecting economic growth and what strategies companies can adopt to make the most of its potential.

Growth Strategies in the Manufacturing Sector

In the manufacturing sector, Generative AI is enabling companies to optimise production processes and accelerate innovation. For example, Generative AI can be used to design more efficient components, reduce product development time and improve final quality. This type of innovation paves the way for more agile and customised production that can respond quickly to market needs.

Impact on Education and Training

Generative AI also has the potential to transform the education and training sector. AI tools can personalise learning paths, provide real-time feedback and facilitate access to high-quality educational content. This can lead to more effective learning and training that is more aligned with the needs of the labour market.

Successful Case Studies

Automotive: Generative AI is used to design safer and more energy-efficient vehicles, reducing costs and development time.

Retail sector: Retailers are using generative AI to personalise the shopping experience, improve inventory management and optimise marketing strategies.

Conclusion

The prospects for growth with Generative AI are huge and varied. Innovation in products and services, operational efficiency and cost reduction, together with successful case studies, illustrate how Generative AI is becoming a key factor for business growth and market expansion. Companies that manage to exploit this technology strategically can expect to gain a significant competitive advantage in their industry.

Practical Approaches

Integrating generative AI into business operations requires a practical and strategic approach. Companies must consider several key factors to ensure effective integration that can lead to successful organisational transformation.

Business Needs Assessment

The first step in integrating generative AI is a thorough assessment of business needs. This process includes identifying areas where AI can provide the greatest benefits, such as automated customer support, effective marketing and business process automation.

Selection of Appropriate Technology

Investing in the right technology is crucial. Companies need to choose Generative AI tools and platforms that align with their specific goals and can integrate seamlessly with existing systems.

Employee Training

Employee training is another crucial aspect. It is essential to develop training programmes to ensure that employees have the necessary skills to work with generative AI and to understand its ethical and legal implications.

Establishing Clear Targets and Metrics

Companies need to establish clear goals and metrics to measure the success of the integration of Generative AI. This helps monitor progress and make adjustments when necessary.

Continuous Monitoring and Adjustment

AI is dynamic. Therefore, it is crucial to continuously monitor the integration of generative AI and be ready to make changes to optimise processes and strategies.

Organisational change planning and management are essential for the successful integration of generative AI in companies. This process requires a holistic approach that considers the impact of technology on all aspects of the organisation.

Strategic Planning

Strategic planning for the integration of generative AI must begin with a clear vision of the business goals and how AI can support them. Companies must establish detailed plans that include technology roadmaps, employee training and process updates.

Communication and Involvement

Effective communication is key to managing organisational change. Companies need to engage employees at all levels, explaining the benefits of Generative AI and how it will affect their work. Employee engagement helps to mitigate resistance and promote faster adoption of the technology.

Skills Development

To make the most of Generative AI, companies need to invest in developing the skills of their employees. This includes training on new tools and processes as well as upgrading existing skills to work effectively with AI.

Change Management

Change management must be proactive and continuous. Companies must monitor the implementation of Generative AI and be ready to adapt to emerging challenges. This may include adjusting plans, resolving technical issues and supporting employees during the transition.

Organisational change management is crucial for the integration of generative AI in companies. This phase requires careful planning and strategic implementation to ensure that the transition to more automated and intelligent systems is smooth and well received within the organisation.

Development of an Innovative Culture

To successfully integrate Generative AI, companies must develop a culture that encourages innovation and acceptance of change. This involves creating an environment where employees feel comfortable exploring new technologies and contributing ideas on how these can be applied to improve business processes.

Ongoing Training and Support

Training is not limited to a single event, but must be a continuous process that supports employees throughout the transition. Companies need to provide educational resources, workshops and training sessions to ensure that all levels of the organisation understand the benefits and potential of Generative AI.

Clear and Transparent Communication

Clear and transparent communication is essential to manage expectations and reduce resistance to change. Companies need to openly communicate the plans for integrating Generative AI, the expected benefits and how these will impact the various roles within the organisation.

CHAPTER 3: GENERATIVE AI INTEGRATION STRATEGIES

The integration of Generative AI requires not only technological and strategic planning, but also a significant commitment to skills development and employee training. This part examines how companies can prepare their staff to work effectively with Generative AI.

Identification of Skills Needed

Companies need to start by identifying the specific skills needed to use generative AI. This may include understanding machine learning models, the ability to interpret the results generated by AI and knowledge of best practices for its implementation.

Customised Training Programmes

Once competencies have been identified, companies need to develop customised training programmes. These programmes should be designed to meet the specific needs of different roles within the organisation and could include both online and classroom training.

Continuous Support and Learning Resources

In addition to initial training, it is essential to provide ongoing support and learning resources for employees. This can include access to communities of practice, webinars, tutorials and online learning platforms that allow employees to stay up-to-date with the latest trends and developments in Generative AI.

Evaluation and Feedback

Companies should regularly evaluate the effectiveness of their training programmes and collect feedback from employees. This helps to identify areas for improvement and to ensure that training is aligned with business objectives and employee needs.

Conclusion

Skills development and training are critical aspects of the integration of Generative AI. By properly preparing employees, companies can maximise the benefits of Generative AI and ensure that their staff are equipped to make the most of this emerging technology.

Generative AI Integration Strategies

After examining planning, change management and competence development, it is essential to focus on consolidation and optimisation post implementation of Generative AI. This final phase ensures that the integration of Generative AI leads to continuous improvements and lasting value for the company.

Consolidation of Changes

Once Generative AI is implemented, companies must consolidate the changes to ensure that they become an integral part of business processes. This includes institutionalising the new practices and ensuring that employees fully adopt them in their daily work.

Performance Monitoring

Continuous performance monitoring is crucial to evaluate the impact of Generative AI. Companies must use clear metrics to measure success, such as increased productivity, reduced costs and improved customer satisfaction.

Continuous Optimisation

Continuous optimisation of generative AI systems is crucial to maintain efficiency and exploit new opportunities. Companies must be prepared to adapt and improve their AI systems based on employee feedback and market developments.

Innovation and Future Development

Finally, companies must look to the future, exploring how Generative AI can support further innovation and the development of new products or services. This may include research and development of new AI applications or expansion into new markets.

Conclusion

Post-implementation consolidation and optimisation. These final steps are crucial to ensure that the integration of Generative AI is not only an immediate success, but also leads to long-term benefits for the company.

Generative AI is revolutionising product design, allowing creators to push traditional boundaries and explore new creative frontiers. This technology offers the ability to rapidly generate virtual prototypes and test a variety of designs efficiently and cost-effectively.

Iterative Design and Experimentation

With Generative AI, designers can experiment with almost infinite iterations of a product in a very short time. This iterative process paves the way for more experimentation and bolder design, pushing the boundaries of innovation.

Customisation on Request

Generative AI also enables on-demand customisation to previously unimaginable levels. Consumers can actively participate in the design process, providing input that AI can use to create tailor-made products that meet their specific needs.

Successful Case Studies

Adidas: Using generative AI, Adidas created the Speedfactory shoe series, which uses automation and customisation to produce high-performance footwear designed for specific customer needs.

Airbus: Airbus is harnessing generative AI to design lighter and stronger aircraft components, improving fuel efficiency and reducing environmental impact.

Conclusion

Product design is just one of the aspects in which Generative AI is bringing innovation and growth. In the next parts, I will continue to explore how Generative AI is affecting manufacturing and what strategies companies are adopting to remain competitive.

Generative AI is transforming the manufacturing sector, making production processes more efficient and flexible. This section examines how Generative AI is optimising production and what strategies companies are adopting to maintain competitiveness.

Advanced Automation

Generative AI is taking automation to a new level, enabling machines to make intelligent decisions in real time. This results in leaner production and reduced downtime, as AI can predict and solve problems before they affect the production line.

Predictive Maintenance

Another key aspect of production optimisation is predictive

maintenance. Generative AI constantly analyses data from machines to predict when faults might occur, enabling preventive interventions that minimise downtime and maximise productivity.

Successful Case Studies

General Electric: GE uses Generative AI to monitor and analyse data from its gas turbines, predicting faults before they happen and optimising maintenance to reduce operating costs.

Siemens: Siemens employs generative AI to create digital simulations of its production processes, allowing operations to be tested and optimised in a virtual environment before implementation in the real world.

Strategies for Maintaining Competitiveness

To remain competitive, companies must adopt strategies that include continuous investment in R&D, training employees to work with new technologies and collaborating with technology partners to stay at the forefront of innovation.

In today's context of rapid technological development, companies need to adopt innovative strategies to harness the potential of Generative AI and maintain competitiveness. This part of the chapter explores how Generative AI can be integrated into business strategies to stimulate innovation and ensure sustainable growth.

Data-driven innovation

Generative AI offers companies the opportunity to use data in new and creative ways. Through predictive analytics and content generation, companies can uncover hidden insights and identify new market opportunities. For example, Generative AI can be used to develop new financial products or customise service offerings based on customer preferences.

Collaboration and Partnership

Strategic partnerships are key to accelerating the adoption of generative AI. By collaborating with universities, technology start-ups and other companies, organisations can access specialist expertise and accelerate the innovation process. These collaborations can also pave the way for new business models and innovative solutions that would not be possible operating in isolation.

Investment in Research and Development

To stay at the forefront, companies need to invest in research and development (R&D). Generative AI requires an ongoing commitment to R&D to explore new applications and improve existing technologies[3]. Investment in R&D can also help companies develop a deep understanding of emerging technologies and position themselves as leaders in their field.

Training and Talent Development

Talent is another key factor for innovation. Companies need to invest in training and developing the skills of their employees to work with Generative AI. This includes not only technical training, but also the development of soft skills such as critical thinking and creative problem solving.

Conclusion

Strategies to drive innovation and maintain competitiveness in the era of Generative AI are multifaceted and require a holistic approach. Data-driven innovation, collaboration and partnerships, investment in R&D and talent training are all essential elements that companies must consider in order to make the most of the opportunities offered by Generative AI.

Strategies to Stimulate Innovation

In the era of Generative AI, companies must adopt innovative strategies to maintain competitiveness and stimulate growth. This part of the chapter explores strategies that companies can implement to harness the potential of Generative AI in improving production and product design.

Incorporating AI into the Creative Process

Generative AI can be used to enrich the creative process, offering new perspectives and solutions that may not be immediately apparent to human eyes. For example, in product design, AI can suggest combinations of materials and shapes that optimise functionality and aesthetics.

Customisation on Request

Generative AI enables on-demand customisation to previously unimaginable levels. Consumers can actively participate in the design process, providing input that AI can use to create tailor-made products that meet their specific needs.

Supply Chain Optimisation

Using generative AI, companies can better predict demand and optimise the supply chain. This not only improves operational efficiency, but also reduces the risk of overproduction or inventory shortages.

Conclusion

Strategies to stimulate innovation and maintain competitiveness in the era of Generative AI are essential for companies seeking to stay ahead of the curve. Incorporating AI into the creative process, customisation and agile manufacturing, and supply chain optimisation are just some of the strategies companies can adopt to harness the potential of Generative AI.

CHAPTER 5: PERSONALISATION AND MARKETING STRATEGIES WITH GENERATIVE AI

Generative AI is revolutionising marketing and the personalisation of the customer experience, offering unprecedented opportunities for companies to connect with their consumers in more meaningful and personalised ways.

Hyper Customisation

Generative AI enables a level of personalisation that goes beyond traditional experiences. Using behavioural and real-time data, companies can create highly contextualised interactions that are relevant to the user at the right time in their journey.

Artificial Intelligence and Customisation

AI customises messages, product and service recommendations for individual users. By analysing data and learning from user behaviour, AI-based tools can create highly personalised encounters that enhance customer experiences and increase engagement.

Effective Strategies for Creating Customised Content

To utilise generative AI in content customisation, it is important to adopt practices such as using multimodal AI for richer content experiences, developing creative prompts and continuously monitoring content performance.

Generative AI is transforming marketing and the personalisation of the customer experience, offering unprecedented opportunities for companies to connect with their consumers in more meaningful and personalised ways.

Insight into Advanced Customisation

With Generative AI, companies can go beyond simple customer segmentation and achieve individual customisation on a large scale. This means that every customer interaction can be unique and customised to that individual's specific context, from their purchasing preferences to their online browsing behaviour.

Examples of Advanced Customisation

Ecommerce: ecommerce platforms are using generative AI to create customised product descriptions that resonate with the specific interests of each customer, thus increasing the chances of conversion.

Streaming services: Services such as Netflix and Spotify use generative AI to personalise recommendations of films, TV series and music playlists, improving user engagement and retention.

Customisation Challenges

Despite the benefits, advanced personalisation presents challenges, including managing data privacy and the need to maintain a balance between personalisation and intrusiveness. Companies must carefully navigate these waters to build trust and maintain positive customer relationships.

The future of digital marketing is closely linked to the evolution of generative AI, which is opening up new avenues for consumer engagement and personalised experiences.

Predictive and Dynamic Marketing

Generative AI is transforming marketing into a more predictive and dynamic business. Companies can use AI models to anticipate customers' needs and offer promotions and content that respond to their behaviour and preferences in real time.

Multi-channel Integration

Generative AI enables a smoother multichannel integration, allowing brands to interact with customers across various digital touchpoints in a consistent and personalised manner. This omnichannel approach is key to building a complete and satisfying customer experience.

Immersive and Interactive Experiences

With generative AI, companies can create immersive and interactive marketing experiences that engage customers in new and engaging ways. This can include augmented reality, personalised video games or virtual shopping experiences that offer an unprecedented level of engagement.

Generative AI is redefining the way companies interact with consumers, offering new ways of engagement that were unimaginable until recently.

Personalised Engagement

Generative AI enables a level of personalised engagement that goes beyond simple demographic or behavioural segmentation. Companies can now interact with customers on a near-individual basis, tailoring messages and experiences in real time to reflect each person's unique needs and preferences.

Artificial Intelligence and Customer Journey

Generative AI can influence every stage of the customer journey, from awareness to purchase to retention. For example, it can be used to automatically generate marketing content that guides customers through the sales funnel, improving conversions and building stronger relationships.

Innovative User Experiences

Companies are leveraging generative AI to create innovative user experiences, such as chatbots that can conduct natural conversations, virtual assistants that offer personalised support or augmented reality platforms that transform the way customers interact with products.

Visions on the Future of Digital Marketing

Looking ahead, Generative AI will continue to play a crucial role in shaping digital marketing. Emerging technologies such as Generative AI are expected to become increasingly integrated into marketing strategies, offering brands new tools to engage customers and remain relevant in a rapidly changing market.

We explored how Generative AI is redefining marketing and personalisation, offering companies new ways to engage and understand their customers. This technology is transforming marketing from an insight-based process to a data-driven one, enabling unprecedented personalisation and creating richer, more engaging user experiences.

Summary of Key Strategies

HyperPersonalisation: Using generative AI to create highly personalised customer experiences, improving engagement and loyalty.

Predictive Marketing: employing AI models to anticipate customer needs and provide relevant content and offers.

Multi-channel integration: Ensure a consistent and customised presence across all digital channels.

Immersive Experiences: Leveraging Generative AI to develop

interactive marketing experiences, such as augmented reality.

Future Implications

Looking ahead, we can expect Generative AI to continue to evolve, offering even more sophisticated tools for digital marketing. Companies adopting these technologies will be better equipped to meet the challenges of a rapidly evolving market and to meet the ever-increasing expectations of consumers.

Companies must now consider how to integrate generative AI into their marketing and personalisation strategies. Investing in this technology is not only about maintaining competitiveness, but also about driving innovation and building deeper and more meaningful relationships with customers.

CHAPTER 6: LEADERSHIP VISIONS AND TALENT MANAGEMENT WITH GENERATIVE AI

Introduction

In the era of generative AI, business leaders must adopt new strategies to guide their organisations through digital transformation. These strategies must focus on integrating AI into business operations and managing talent in a technologically advanced environment.

Adapting to Change

Leaders must be agile and adaptable to navigate rapid technological change. This requires a deep understanding of how generative AI can be applied to improve business processes and create new business opportunities.

Development of an AICentric Vision

It is crucial that leaders develop an AIcentric vision for their company, identifying how Generative AI can support long-term goals and drive innovation.

Promoting a Culture of Lifelong Learning

To remain competitive, leaders must foster a culture of continuous learning within their organisations, encouraging employees to develop new skills and adapt to emerging technologies.

Talent Management and Development

In today's technologically advanced environment, talent

management and development have become more complex and crucial to business success. Generative AI offers new opportunities to address these challenges and to strengthen the capabilities of the workforce.

Talent Identification and Development

Companies need to identify the key talent needed to work effectively with generative AI and develop targeted training programmes. This can include learning new technical skills, as well as adapting to new models of collaborative working and decision-making.

Culture of Continuous Learning

A culture of continuous learning is essential to support innovation and adaptability. Companies must provide learning and development platforms that enable employees to constantly update their skills in response to evolving technologies.

Leadership in Change

Leaders must be champions of change, promoting the adoption of generative AI and driving cultural transformation. They must be role models in learning and using AI, demonstrating the value this technology can bring.

Retention Strategies

As the labour market evolves, retention strategies become crucial. Companies need to create attractive career paths and offer professional development opportunities that align individual goals with corporate goals.

New Frontiers in Talent Management

We explore new frontiers in talent management that Generative

AI is opening for business leaders, focusing on how they can exploit these opportunities to remain competitive.

Integrating AI into Talent Development

Generative AI can be used to identify optimal career paths for employees, customising development plans according to their skills and aspirations. This datadriven approach enables more targeted and effective talent management.

Improving Diversity and Inclusion

Generative AI can help overcome unconscious bias in recruitment and talent management, promoting greater diversity and inclusion. By analysing performance data without bias, AI can identify and promote talent based solely on merit.

Conclusion

We explored new strategies that business leaders can adopt to manage and develop talent in the age of generative AI. These strategies will help companies take advantage of the opportunities offered by AI to improve talent management and remain competitive.

CHAPTER 7: SUSTAINABILITY STRATEGIES AND SOCIAL RESPONSIBILITY WITH GENERATIVE AI

Social and Environmental Impact

Introduction

Generative AI is having a profound impact not only on the technological landscape, but also on the social and environmental ones. Its applications can bring significant benefits, but also present challenges that require a responsible and sustainable approach.

Social Impact of Generative AI

Generative AI has the potential to improve collaboration, content creation and knowledge sharing among social impact organisations, enabling the sector to learn and evolve collectively. However, it is crucial to carefully assess the social impacts of these systems to avoid damages such as reinforcing stereotypes or creating inequalities.

Environmental Impact of Generative AI

Generative AI can entail significant environmental costs, especially in terms of energy consumption and water use. The formation of large AI models requires a considerable amount of electricity, which can lead to increased carbon emissions if not managed in a sustainable manner.

Strategies for Responsible Innovation

To meet these challenges, companies must adopt responsible

innovation strategies that include:

Prioritisation of Data Quality: Focus on data quality rather than quantity, to develop more efficient and less resource-intensive AI models.

Balancing Model Size and Efficiency: Avoid the uncontrolled increase in the size of AI models and instead focus on domain-specific models that optimise resources and address use cases efficiently.

Developing Energy Efficient Infrastructure: Invest in infrastructure that reduces the energy consumption and environmental impact of data centres and AI processes.

Generative AI, although offering significant advantages in terms of efficiency and innovation, also brings with it environmental and social challenges that require special attention.

Environmental Challenges

The formation and operation of generative AI models require a large amount of energy, which raises concerns in terms of energy consumption and environmental impact. Companies must therefore consider energy efficiency and the use of renewable energy when implementing these technologies.

Responsible Innovation

To mitigate environmental impact, companies can adopt responsible innovation strategies, such as:

Energy Efficiency: Optimise energy use in data centres, e.g. through improved cooling and the use of more efficient hardware.

Sustainability: Integrate sustainability considerations in the early stages of product development, ensuring that Generative AI is used in a way that supports corporate sustainability goals.

Research and Development: Investing in R&D to develop new generative AI technologies that are less resource-intensive and more environmentally friendly.

Examples of Responsible Innovation

Google DeepMind: Using AI to optimise cooling in its data centres, Google reduced energy consumption by 40 per cent.

IBM: IBM is developing new AI models that require less data and computational power for training, thus reducing the environmental impact.

Strategies for Responsible Innovation

In the era of generative AI, companies are called upon to explore new strategies to ensure that innovation is responsible and sustainable. This means carefully considering the social and environmental impact of AI technologies and adopting practices that promote long-term benefits.

Sustainability in Core Business

Companies need to integrate sustainability into the core business, ensuring that the use of generative AI is aligned with global sustainability goals. This includes reducing the carbon footprint, using resources efficiently and supporting biodiversity.

Ethics and Generative AI

Ethics play a key role in responsible innovation. Companies must develop and follow ethical guidelines for the use of generative AI, ensuring that technologies are used in a fair and non-discriminatory manner.

Collaboration for Sustainability

Collaboration between companies, governments and non-governmental organisations is essential to promote responsible innovation. These partnerships can help develop common standards and share best practices for the sustainable use of generative AI.

CONCLUSION

As we close the pages of this exploratory journey through Generative AI and its transformative impact on business, we stand at the dawn of a new era. We have explored how Generative AI is redefining business models, stimulating growth, integrating innovative business operations, and shaping the future of digital marketing. We also discussed the strategies leaders must adopt to navigate this new landscape and how talent management must evolve in a technologically advanced environment.

FINAL REFLECTIONS

Generative AI is not only a driving force for efficiency and automation; it is a catalyst for human innovation and creativity.

Growth supported by Generative AI is not only about financial gains, but also about social enrichment and environmental progress.

Leadership in the age of generative AI requires a bold vision, a commitment to continuous learning and a deep understanding of the human impact of technology.

Social responsibility and sustainability must be at the heart of every Generative AI initiative, ensuring that while we build the future, we also protect our planet and its people.

CALL TO ACTION

This book is a call to action for business leaders, practitioners and innovators in every industry. It is a call to harness Generative AI not only for business success, but also to drive positive change in the world. As we move forward, we must do so with care, consideration and a commitment to ethics and responsibility.

www.ingramcontent.com/pod-product-compliance
Lightning Source LLC
Chambersburg PA
CBHW030058230526
45471CB00003B/1151